BRIGHT NOTES

CRY, THE BELOVED COUNTRY AND OTHER WORKS BY ALAN PATON

Intelligent Education

Nashville, Tennessee

BRIGHT NOTES: Cry, The Beloved Country and Other Works
www.BrightNotes.com

No part of this publication may be used or reproduced in any manner whatsoever without written permission, except in the case of brief quotations in critical articles and reviews. For permissions, contact Influence Publishers http://www.influencepublishers.com.

ISBN: 978-1-645420-02-6 (Paperback)
ISBN: 978-1-645420-03-3 (eBook)

Published in accordance with the U.S. Copyright Office Orphan Works and Mass Digitization report of the register of copyrights, June 2015.

Originally published by Monarch Press.
Connor P. Hartnett, 1965
2020 Edition published by Influence Publishers.

Interior design by Lapiz Digital Services. Cover Design by Thinkpen Designs.

Printed in the United States of America.

Library of Congress Cataloging-in-Publication Data forthcoming.
Names: Intelligent Education
Title: BRIGHT NOTES: Cry, The Beloved Country and Other Works
Subject: STU004000 STUDY AIDS / Book Notes

CONTENTS

1) Introduction to Alan Paton   1

2) Introduction to Cry, The Beloved Country   13

3) Critical Analysis   15

4) Character Analyses   30

5) Review of Criticism   41

6) Essay Questions and Answers   47

7) Introduction to Too Late The Phalarope   49

8) Review of Criticism   56

9) Essay Questions and Answers   58

10) A Troubled Land   60

11) Bibliography   66

INTRODUCTION TO ALAN PATON

South Africa, its peoples, and its problems are the subjects of Alan Paton's two novels, *Cry, the Beloved Country* and *Too Late the Phalarope*, and his collection of short stories, *Tales from a Troubled Land*. His fiction reflects his wide knowledge of the many races and cultures of the Union of South Africa and his understanding of the problems and aspirations of the various groups in his native land. South Africa is overwhelmingly a nation of native Africans, but it is ruled by a white minority of European descent. The whites are made up of two groups. The English-speaking whites have a strong attachment to Britain and the Crown. The Afrikaners, people speaking a language derived from Dutch, have strong anti-British feelings and a marked sense of their own national identity. These two groups have traditionally regarded one another with either suspicion or hatred.

Paton was born January 11, 1903, in Pietermaritzburg in the English-speaking province of Natal, but his parents taught him to feel sympathy for the language and cultural struggle of the Afrikaners. His father was a civil-service employee and his mother a school teacher. Both were pious Anglicans. The piety he learned from his parents and their understanding of the Afrikaners are reflected in Paton's fiction. Both the Rev. Stephen Kumalo and the murdered Arthur Jarvis in *Cry, the Beloved*

Country are pious Anglicans. Pieter van Vlaanderen in *Too Late the Phalarope* is not saintly, but he is pious. Pieter is an Afrikaner, a member of the Dutch Reformed Church and his life in an Afrikaner community is told with sympathy and understanding. Paton never heard Afrikaans spoken as a child, but he learned it as a young man. He praises the suppleness and beauty of this language. When Paton's education was completed, he learned Zulu, the African language spoken in Natal, and he acquired a knowledge of other African languages and cultures.

Paton was educated in Pietermaritzburg and constantly broadened his understanding of his own country. He finished his high school education at Martzburg College School in 1918 and then attended the University of Natal. He was active in the dramatic and religious societies and one year won the five mile race. He says that at this time he walked over every section of Natal with college friends, usually traveling thirty miles a day. At the University of Natal he learned to sympathize with the aspirations of the native Africans, the Coloreds (people of mixed blood), and the Indians. He excelled in both mathematics and English. After he earned a Bachelor of Science degree in 1922, he returned to the University to specialize in English, and he earned a Bachelor of Education degree in 1924.

On leaving the University of Natal, Paton became a teacher in a Zulu school in the country village of Ixopo. He used this setting in *Cry, the Beloved Country*. The village of Ndotsheni near the Drakenberg Mountains, where the Reverend Kumalo has his parish, is located near Ixopo. In 1928 Paton married Doris Olive Francis and the same year he took a post as teacher in his native Pietermaritzburg. He left this position in 1935 to become Principal of Diepkloof Reformatory near Johannesburg in Transvaal Province. The reformatory had just been transferred from the Department of Prisons to the Department of Education.

Paton transformed this grim penal institution into a modern training school. His chief means of rewarding or punishing the boys was by giving or withholding more freedom to move about. There were at that time between 600 and 750 boys in the institution. It is the largest institution of its kind on the African continent. Because of Paton's valuable work with these boys, the Department of Education refused to give him leave of absence to enlist in the army when war broke out in Europe in 1939. The account of Absalom Kumalo's stay in a reformatory near Johannesburg in *Cry, the Beloved Country* and most of the stories in *Tales from a Troubled Land*, especially "Sponono" and "The Death of a Totsi," are based on this experience. He was recognized as a leading authority in South Africa on corrective institutions. Towards the end of the war, he visited prisons and reformatories in Sweden, Norway, England, the United States, Canada, and other countries in order to study their methods.

While visiting Trondheim, Norway, Paton began to write *Cry, the Beloved Country*. He finished it in San Francisco and it was published in New York in 1948. It was very well received. James Stern wrote in the *New Republic* that it was "probably . . . one of the best novels of our time." The same year Paton left the Diepkloof Reformatory and went to live on the southern coast of Natal. He wrote many articles on South African affairs, took part in many kinds of activities, and devoted some time to his two hobbies, bird watching and gardening. The nameless principal of the reformatory in Paton's short stories also has a passion for gardening. Pieter van Vlaanderen in *Too Late the Phalarope* is very interested in plants and flowers and both Pieter and his father are bird watchers.

In 1951 Paton and his wife moved to the Toc H Tuberculosis Settlement. Mr. Arthur Jarvis and his wife, in *Cry, the Beloved Country*, were invited to visit Toc H. Here Paton was responsible for the training of African natives who were suffering from tuberculosis so that on discharge they would be equipped to earn a living. He was called to London in 1951 for consultation on the filming of *Cry, the Beloved Country*. He then began to write *Too Late the Phalarope*, and it was published in 1955. *Tales from a Troubled Land* was published in 1961. He also wrote nonfiction. *Hope for South Africa*, for example, which was published in 1958, gives a historical explanation of the complex cultural and racial problems of the Union of South Africa. It also outlines the solutions offered by the Liberal Party of South Africa. Paton was one of the founders of the Liberal Association of South Africa. This later developed into the Liberal Party and Paton became its President. For American high school boys and girls, he wrote *The Land and the People of South Africa* (1955). Paton was active in the Non-European Boys' Club while at Diepkloof Reformatory. He was later elected the Club's President. Arthur Jarvis in *Cry, the Beloved Country* is President of a similar organization, the Claremont African Boys' Club.

Three of Paton's works of fiction have been adapted for the stage. *Cry, the Beloved Country* was presented as a musical play in New York in 1949 under the title *Lost in the Stars*. Maxwell Anderson wrote the words for the play and Kurt Weill wrote the music. Paton adapted *Too Late the Phalarope* for the stage and it was presented in New York in 1956. *Sponono*, which is based on a short story of the same name, was given in New York in 1963. Krishna Shah helped Paton write this play.

Paton has received wide recognition for his novels and for his efforts on behalf of the native population of the Union of South Africa. Yale University gave him the honorary degree of Doctor of Humane Letters in 1954. He was given the American Freedom Award in 1960 and in 1961 the Award from the Free Academy of Art in Hamburg, Germany.

SOUTH AFRICAN BACKGROUND

The prime cause of social injustice in the fiction of Alan Paton is apartheid. This Afrikaans word means "separateness" or "segregation." Apartheid is very much like the practice of racial segregation in the American South. In the United States it is the policy of the federal government to remove discrimination and racial segregation. In the Union of South Africa, however, the official policy is to make laws that will bring about more and more segregation. Supporters of apartheid look forward to the day when Africans of different tribes, Coloreds, Indians, and whites will be living in absolutely separate communities, work at separate jobs, and be educated in entirely separate school systems. Supporters of apartheid claim that they wish to protect the African's cultural integrity and tribal society.

Alan Paton and others who are opposed to the doctrine of apartheid deny all these claims. They say that white civilization and the South African industrial society have already destroyed forever the African tribal system. On attempting to separate the races, they claim, it is almost always the non-European (African, Colored, Indian) who suffers property loss, almost never the European or white. In giving separate jobs to the various races, whites receive the best ones and the lowest type of work is given to other races. The educational system of the non-Europeans is also very much inferior to that of whites. Opponents also point out that apartheid humiliates and restricts the non-European. At present the whites, who are a small minority, have most of the land and wealth. They claim, moreover, that apartheid cannot work because it is too expensive and because the South African economy is based on non-European labor.

The policy, but not the name, of apartheid was first established in South Africa in the 1770s. The Dutch ancestors of the Afrikaners were then pushing northward from the Cape of Good Hope and began to settle in the land of Xosas. These warlike African natives were, like the Afrikaners, cattle owners and a very determined people, but spears were no match for the guns of the Europeans. Since that time the attitude of the Afrikaner has remained inflexible, but the effectiveness of his racial policy changed as he encountered new peoples. His policy was also affected by changes in sovereignty. The Dutch East India Company established a rest station for Dutch trading vessels in Capetown in 1602, but it was not until 1657 that the Company permitted Dutchmen to take and farm land on the Cape. South Africa at that time was inhabited by the primitive Hottentots and Bushmen. They were few in number and were almost wiped out when infected by smallpox. West African slaves were imported the same year that Dutchmen began to farm on the Cape of Good Hope. Later Malaysian slaves were imported. Marriage between whites and blacks was at first acceptable. A new racial group, the Cape Coloreds, was produced by a mingling of Hottentots, Malays, and white settlers and sailors. There are over 1,300,000 Cape Coloreds today and almost all of them speak Afrikaans.

When large numbers of Dutch, German, and French settlers joined the original Dutch, interracial marriage was no longer approved. The racial attitude of the Afrikaner hardened and, like the whites in the American South, they believed that the Bible said that the various races were not equal and that races should not be mixed. The Afrikaners' sense of cultural identity or exclusiveness also developed as their original Dutch language began to change to reflect their experiences in Africa and the contributions of the Germans and French immigrants whom they absorbed. This modified Dutch was later to be called Afrikaans and it eventually replaced Dutch as the language of culture and instruction. These land-hungry farmers and cattlemen slowly moved northward until they had settlements as far north as present-day Rhodesia and Southwest Africa.

Attempts by both Dutch and English governments to contain these people proved a failure. They defied their Governor van Plettenberg in 1778 when they crossed the Fish River and entered the territory of the Xosas in Eastern Cape Province. The British occupied the Cape of Good Hope in 1795 and in the early 1800s British missionaries and colonizers followed British administrators. The missionaries outraged the Afrikaners by preaching racial equality and brotherhood and the administrators angered them further by granting civil rights to the Cape Coloreds and by insisting that white farmers be punished if they mistreated their servants or slaves. In 1836 many Afrikaners, disgusted by the British land and racial policy, defied the ban on further invasions of tribal land and made a great migration to the north.

This migration is called the Great Trek. Because the Afrikaners were for the most part an agricultural people, they were also called Boers, as this means "farmers" in their language. The Boers, or Afrikaners, established a republic in 1838 in what is now Natal Province. The British annexed this territory shortly afterwards, and most of the Afrikaners moved on into what is now Transvaal Province. Natal was to remain in the hands of English-speaking settlers.

The newly established Boer republics of Transvaal and Orange Free State were given a formal promise by the British government that their freedom and integrity would not be violated. These promises were broken when diamonds and gold were discovered. Diamonds were discovered near Kimberley in Orange Free State in 1866 and shortly thereafter the British annexed that part of Orange Free State. Transvaal was annexed in

1877, but the Afrikaners revolted and the British granted them freedom in all matters except foreign relations. The Afrikaners in the Transvaal were threatened again when gold was discovered in 1886. They were almost completely surrounded by British colonies and feared further British moves. Dr. Starr Jameson, a friend of Cecil Rhodes, Prime Minister of the British Cape Colony, raided the Transvaal in 1895 in order to give the British an excuse to invade. Following this and other provocations, the republics of Transvaal and Orange Free State declared war on Britain in 1899. This war, the so-called Boer War, ended in British victory in 1902, and both republics were made British colonies. In 1910 Cape Province, Natal, Orange Free State, and Transvaal were united to form the Union of South Africa.

Afrikaners gained control of the Union of South Africa and then set about to reverse British cultural and racial policies. With great bitterness, they refer to the century of British interference with their freedom, culture, and racial policy as the "Century of Wrongs." Over 60 per cent of South African whites are Afrikaners and their control over the government is further strengthened by voting laws which give proportionally more representation to the rural areas than to the urban areas. Most white farmers in South Africa are Afrikaners. English had been the sole official language of South Africa under British rule; the Afrikaners made Afrikaans one of the two official languages. All South African prime ministers since the formation of the Union have been Afrikaners. General Louis Botha, who brought South Africa into World War I on behalf of Britain, and General Jan Christiaan Smuts, who brought the Union into World War II, favored a policy of reconciliation between English-speaking and Afrikaans-speaking peoples.

Other Afrikaners regarded this policy as a betrayal of their nation and followed General Hertzog when he broke away from the Union Party of Botha in 1912 to form the Nationalist Party.

Jakob van Vlaanderen, the father in *Too Late the Phalarope*, is a supporter of the Nationalist Party and cannot understand how his own son Pieter could fight in a war for England, the enemy nation. The Nationalist Party has been in power without a break since 1948. It has been their policy to bring about, by law, a complete separation of races. Several thousand Cape Coloreds and Africans had the right to vote in Cape Province when the Union was formed, but Coloreds and Africans could not vote in the other provinces. However, in the Cape only whites could be members of Parliament. In 1936 the Nationalists removed all Africans from the common voting register and in 1951 all Cape Coloreds were removed. Four white members represent them in Parliament. They cannot vote for or against candidates representing whites.

In order to carry out the apartheid policy, Parliament enacted legislation designed to remove the various races to separate areas, to separate them in schools, churches, and jobs. It is assumed that the permanent homes of the Africans are in the native reserves or reservations. Africans, however, own only 16 per cent of the land and it is generally semi-arid or ruined by poor farming methods. Yet Africans number nearly 10,000,000 and constitute over 65 per cent of the population of South Africa. South Africa has large industries, rich mines, and a large urban population. Most of the menial work in the factories, mines, and urban areas is done by Africans. Yet Africans are not considered permanent residents of places where they work. They must show a pass (permit) in order to move to a city and may be sent back to the native reserve by a white government official. In spite of this and the fact that the government restricts more and more jobs to whites, more Africans are moving to the urban areas.

Government officials may also classify people by race. A colored man may be classified by a government official as an African and his sons as Coloreds. Family life among non-Europeans is hurt by poor housing. Africans and other non-Europeans may find after they have managed to build decent homes that the government will declare the area in which they live a white area and they will have to move, probably to a slum. Whites may not enter certain African areas without permission, and Africans must have a pass to move about or to reside outside of the native reserve. The pass laws are regularly broken. Stephanie in *Too Late the Phalarope* returns to her native reserve without permission and is reprimanded for it by Pieter van Vlaanderen. There are no reserves for Coloreds and Indians, but the government is working to assign special areas to them. Most of the choice land and the larger areas of the cities and towns are earmarked for whites.

In both Paton's novels these apartheid laws have tragic consequences. Absalom Kumalo and Arthur Jarvis die because of the wall that has been put between the races. Pieter van Vlaanderen is destroyed by prejudice and by a law which makes it a criminal offense for a white and a black to have sexual relations.

REALISM

Paton is primarily a realistic writer. He generally writes about ordinary people and his descriptions of people, cities, and landscapes appear to be accurate. His people generally speak the way ordinary people would speak and the events in his stories appear to be possible. Because of his special experience, Paton's descriptions of the slums of Johannesburg and the workings of police and reformatory officials and courts seem especially accurate. His novels, in different degrees, concern themselves with the effect of society on the lives of individuals and describe the way society operates. This applies in a real way to *Cry, the Beloved Country*. Novels with such emphasis are called problem, or sociological, novels. In theory, a realistic writer presents his material to his reader without comment of interpretation. Paton's purpose is quite different. *Cry, the Beloved Country* resembles in some ways Harriet Beecher Stowe's *Uncle Tom's Cabin*. Mrs. Stowe's novel, which was published in 1852, describes the evils of slavery in the United States before the Civil War. It was an attempt to arouse public opinion against slavery. Paton's purpose is to make men aware of the evils of apartheid. *Too Late the Phalarope* is also concerned with the evils of apartheid, but its primary focus is on the mind and heart of Pieter van Vlaanderen and those things within his nature which cause him to act in certain ways.

LITERARY TECHNIQUES

In *Cry, the Beloved Country*, with some exceptions, the story is told from the point of view of the omniscient, or all-knowing, author. *Too Late the Phalarope* is told entirely by a third party. An omniscient author knows what all the characters in a novel are thinking and doing. Paton, for example, knows and tells the reader what Mrs. Lithebe thinks of the Rev. Stephen Kumalo. A third party is anyone besides the author. When a writer gives us the conversation of his characters, he does not claim to know what they are thinking. He is merely acting as a reporter. Mrs. Seme's search for a place to live is, for the most part, reported without any indication of her thoughts. James Jarvis finds and reads the manuscript of a speech his son Arthur wrote. Even though the views of Arthur Jarvis are exactly those of Alan Paton, it is not Paton the omniscient author, but a third party Arthur Jarvis, who speaks. There is no omniscient author in *Too Late the Phalarope*. Here Paton has again used the technique of the discovered manuscript. The whole novel is supposedly written by Tante Sophie, a third person. Even when Tante Sophie tells the thoughts of her nephew Pieter van Vlaanderen, she is not omniscient. She is quoting from the diary and other papers he gave her.

SYMBOLS

Both novels are dominated by the symbol of a bird. In *Cry, the Beloved Country*, the titihoya represents the land of South Africa. It has deserted the veld, or prairie, around Ndotsheni because that land has been destroyed by primitive farming methods. It still lives on the uplands where there are rich farms. The titihoya cries aloud to the people to love and take care of their land. This love makes a man afraid because of the sickness of the soil and the injustice of apartheid in South Africa. In *Too Late the Phalarope*, the phalarope, a rare sea bird not native to South Africa, represents understanding and love between people. It is seldom seen and it is found too late.

INTRODUCTION TO CRY, THE BELOVED COUNTRY

AUTHOR'S NOTE

Alan Paton pays tribute to two South Africans who had worked for racial equality there, and he thanks two Americans who helped him publish this novel. Both Professor R. F. Hoernle and Sir Ernest Oppenheimer were Germans who emigrated to South Africa. Professor Hoernle, who died in 1943, five years before this novel was published, had been Professor of Philosophy at the University of Witwatersrand in Transvaal Province. He fought to protect the rights of the Africans. The Reverend Msimangu says that Professor Hoernle had brains, courage, a beautiful voice, and could always win an argument because his facts were right. This standard will be used throughout the novel in judging such characters as John Kumalo, Dubula, Tomlinson, and Arthur Jarvis as leaders of Africa.

Sir Ernest Oppenheimer, who died in 1957, nine years after the novel was published, acquired great wealth in diamonds, gold, and other minerals in South Africa. He was worth several million dollars at the time of his death. Even though he got this wealth in a South African economy based on cheap African labor, he strongly favored a more liberal racial policy in South

Africa. His son, Harry Frederick Oppenheimer, inherited both his father's wealth and his father's liberal views on race.

Paton dedicated his novel to Mr. and Mrs. Aubrey Burns of Fairfax, California, because they first read his novel, had it typed, and approached publishers for him. When Paton wrote this novel, the population of Johannesburg was about 750,000. Today it is over 1,000,000 and it is growing rapidly. In 1948 there were about 10,000,000 people in South Africa. Today there are almost 16,000,000. The Afrikaner population is increasing faster than the English-speaking population because of a higher birthrate. For the same reason, the African population is growing faster than the whites.

CRY, THE BELOVED COUNTRY

CRITICAL ANALYSIS

Within a few lines of entering *Cry, the Beloved Country*, the reader becomes aware that an enchanted spell is being cast. The source of this spell is the language of the book itself. It creates a continuous tonal background throughout the novel and at the same time, it constitutes the means by which the story and its purposes are not merely observed, but experienced. Flowing lyrically in narrative and meditative passages, the language becomes brittle with the anxious and defensive statements of the fearful upholders of the white status quo; moves haltingly and painfully through a funeral; and proceeds with implacable measure through a judgement of death. Taking as many forms as there are people and actions in the book, the language remains, nevertheless consistent, reflecting the unity of style which has its source in the author.

THE HUMAN LEVEL

While the language gives wholeness and form to the novel, it also reflects the many-leveled structure of the book. There are the people - the human level. From one aspect, the characters are actors in a parable. From another, they exist as individuals living through an interval in their lives. From this aspect, the characters are unique personalities who have come into contact with each other through their actions and the actions of those important to them, and whose lives are shaken, and in some cases changed, by that contact. They are also individuals subject to their environment; to their past which has conditioned them, and to the moment, which both moves them and is affected by them. For they are also the shapers of their world; they have created it in measure and continue to change it as they move through it. And they are the children of what we call for want of a more precise word, fate, that combination of apparently purposeless incident and accident that Paton calls "secret" and whose mysterious effects we call "the human condition." But above all, each character of the novel is a unique person, with an appearance and interior life all his own, not to be found again anywhere else in the novel or in the world.

THE POLITICAL LEVEL

On the political level of the novel we consider the pros and cons of the conditions of the environment, as we are presented with different views of their causes and with alternatives to the solution of the problems they create. Paton presents these aspects of the novel in various forms. Simple descriptive passages of conditions under which no human being can live with dignity, are contrasted with passages describing conditions under which a few live very well. Carefully thought-out essays of the humanitarian, Arthur Jarvis, as they are read after Arthur's death by his father provide another tone. And the anxious musings and statements of anonymous individuals who are identified in the novel convey yet another mood. But the conditions are always the same: there is a white, powerful, integrated minority whose comfortable economic conditions and status are provided by the labor of a black and colored, disintegrated majority who live for the most part in profound economic and social deprivation. The white minority-one-fifth of the population-is fearful, and the native majority-twelve million people-is restive. There the agreement ends. Whether this state is desirable or undesirable, whether it should be changed, what this change should be, and how the changes can and should be made-on these matters there are a hundred voices, and at least a dozen speak in *Cry, the Beloved Country*.

THE PHILOSOPHY

There is still another level, deep and resonant which gives its power to the book. We can call it philosophical, **metaphysical**, or spiritual-whatever word we choose to describe the nature of man and his relation to the universe. But for Paton, these considerations are not dealt with merely as a set of thoughtful abstractions, although the novel is rich with observations and ideas about these mysteries. They are implicit in the cries of the characters of the novel as they confront painful and puzzling events. They are explicit in Arthur Jarvis' essays, in Stephen Kumalo's inner monologues, and in the narrative passages of the novel. The author concretizes these metaphysical questions in a South African world, but the abstractions he deals with are of universal concern. For, to Paton, the problem of South Africa is not merely a problem between white and black; between a powerful minority and an oppressed majority; between the results of history and the needs of the future. Even though these problems are also world-wide, they are only symptomatic of the deeper problems of man. Paton considers two fundamental problems: one is the abyss of fear-of loss of status, wealth, comfort, and even life-which lies between the ideal which man desires and the reality which is all he can achieve-a reality where love and hate appear unpredictably, where two men rarely meet as equals, and where abundance is as elusive as rain in drought. The other basic human problem dealt with in the novel is the element of chance, of coincidence and accident, against which no man can protect himself. Thus, on the philosophical level, *Cry the Beloved Country* is the story of the struggle of man with fear and fate, and how, out of his inner character, he rises above them or succumbs to their power.

PEOPLE AND CHOICE

But there is still another level on which the novel proceeds concurrently with all the others, and here the human and the spiritual meld, so that we view individuals and whole societies in their struggles with fear and fate. We watch each character respond to the people and events which touch him, and make choices which determine his life. And although Paton acknowledges that the results of all choices are only partial in their effectiveness and that future problems may lie beyond all solutions, there is yet a moral in this novel: that the power of fear can only be overcome by the power of love. And so it is in the novel. Where fear wins, there is destruction, even if it is only pain for a moment at harsh words. Where love wins, there is happiness and growth. But ultimately, the novel shows, it is acts motivated by love of individuals that bridge the gap between the ideal and the real.

Of course, when speaking of separate levels of a novel, it cannot be imagined that these can be actually disassembled in separate parts. Rather, we have separated various strains which thread through the novel in order to understand them more clearly. But it is only as an integrated whole that a work can be fully experienced.

LANGUAGE AND STYLE AS CONTENT

The Logic of Praise

As we have noted, the language and style in which *Cry, the Beloved Country* is written both form the background and contribute to the structure of the novel. The nature of this background, or tone, is closely related to the author's thesis of the supremacy of love, for it is a tone of "praise" in the biblical sense. This tone is set by the first lines as they describe the hills above the valley of Umzimkulu, as and it continues to the last. Since this is praise in the biblical sense, it is not the praise of approval but that of affirmation, the affirmation of that life which Paton views as the manifestation of God. According to this belief, all life is good, not in the sense that it is directly beneficial, but that it is valuable. It presumes further, that the standard of value by which life is to be appraised is not man's, but God's. However, God's standards are not known to us - they are "a secret." Then, once we accept Paton's thesis that God is all-loving, we must also accept the fact that His standards, by which the value of life in all its manifestations is set, must also be good. Therefore, it is not up to individuals to pick and choose what aspects of life they consider valuable, and what aspects are valueless. Consequently Paton's approach to life is that all life is valuable, and his religion demands that he give expression to his belief in the form of praise.

Praise as Compassion

This is accomplished in the novel in a number of ways. There is a general absence of adjectives which involve value judgments: scenes and individuals are described in objective terms. For example, instead of describing an eroded landscape in terms of "waste" and "destruction," he uses such terms as "dry" and "bare." In describing people who have undesirable qualities, he also avoids value words; instead he describes them in terms of their outward appearances and behavior, and lets them speak for themselves. He seems to be aware of why people behave as they do, and if they behave badly, he views them with regret rather than distaste; as ground down by their own fear, a fear made great by their circumstances. We recognize this attitude as compassion, an attitude which is based on understanding. Understanding is incompatible with hate; it rises only from love, and we love only what we value. Using this logic, one can see that the compassionate tone in which the novel is written truly reflects a profound humanitarianism, an appreciation of the value of man and nature because it is. In this light, it can be seen that a belief in God is not prerequisite to the appreciation of the novel. Although the author's attitude grows out of his religious belief, it is expressed in a concern for man in the world, a concern all readers can share.

However, the means by which Paton has accomplished this do not lie merely in the use of objective description, but in other aspects of Paton's language: simplicity of line, biblical phrasing, enumeration or cataloging, and a constantly shifting point of view. All of these devices are so integrated into the structure of the novel that they actually contribute to its progress and to the reader's apprehension of the events, as well as to his experience of compassion.

Simplicity of Line

The simplicity of line is important because it is an effective way of achieving that directness of feeling which characterizes actual human speech, and thus contributes to the feeling quality of the book itself. This simplicity is not only evident in the dialogue, but in the narrative passages and the interior and exterior monologues in which the book abounds. We can open the book at random to find examples. For instance, action is described in simple, direct statements of subject and predicate with a minimum of abstract modifiers. The only modification is the use of adjectival and adverbial modifying clauses and simple, telling adjectives. The author's style also includes compound sentences, but these mostly comprise simple sentences joined by a conjunction. On the other hand, there is very little inversion and all the other devices which constitute the structure of elegant style, while **metaphors** are almost completely lacking. But the very simplicity gives the prose a directness and honesty which is in itself an argument for the book's theme.

Direct Address

In part because of this simplicity of line, Paton is able to switch easily to a form of narrative which uses direct address: using the pronoun "you" with the present tense rather than the third person passive. By means of this device, Paton draws the reader in, forces him to engage himself in the story, to participate in the events and share Paton's compassion for the characters.

Biblical Phrasing

Another form of narration, which the author uses to comment on the action, is directly derived from the Bible. There are entire sections that have the quality of the Psalms. In using these forms which are so directly derived from the Bible, Paton accomplishes a great deal. On the one hand, he completely avoids the difficulty of objectively describing feelings and events, which, because of their depth or violence, are difficult for the reader to experience, both because he does not want to experience them, and because at the moment of reading, they are far away from the reader's immediate reality. They are also difficult to describe objectively in simple language because the "heavy" words have been overused by the mass media, and it is hard to give them their due power while avoiding triteness. But biblical terminology is connected in the Western world with profound events-with birth, marriage, rites of inauguration, and death. Thus their use evokes at least awe, and a sense that one is in the presence of something solemn and important. However, we must note that it is not the use of the device, alone, but the language which is employed that creates the effect.

Enumeration

The technique of enumeration, whereby a scene is created by cataloging the items or events that comprises it is also used in Bible, but its derivation in the English language is not primarily biblical. Writers as disparate as Swift and Thomas Wolfe have used it effectively, and there is hardly an English novel which does not employ it. Paton, however, uses it in his own way, creating with it not merely images of place, but also of space and time. For example, he gives the reader a sense of the great distance that lies between the town of Ndotsheni and the city of Johannesburg by enumerating the towns and the scenery through which the traveler passes in prose which has a cinematic quality. We are not merely presented with careful catalogue, but to language which reflects the alternations of the countryside - now desolate, now beautiful. When the reader "arrives" in the bewilderment of Johannesburg, a great space has been encompassed.

In the same way, Paton uses the device of enumeration to express action. He takes the reader through the action step by step. But through his careful selection of the elements presented, he also conveys the emotion of the action, so that the reader can perceive the meaning of the experience involved.

To see how important Paton's artistry is in making his device meaningful, we have only to turn to the part where James Jarvis, Arthur's father, sits reading his son's writings. The tone is completely different from that of the preceding passage. When we read the passage in its entirety, we note how slowly and haltingly it is paced, and how the rhythm of the sentences is repetitive, so that a monotonous effect is achieved.

Appropriateness

This paragraph is also an excellent example of Paton's ability to adapt his language to both the situation and the character. We have observed how the author changes the pace and tone of his language to express the emotion inherent in the situation. This effect is also achieved in the novel by the repetition of sentence pattern, where each sentence is a compound of two or more simple sentences, rather than a repetition of rhythm. By this means Paton achieves the easy pace of restfulness, rather than the dull monotony of despair.

Paton's appropriateness of language also is used to differentiate character and race. The speech of Kumalo and Msimangu is of course partly conditioned by the fact that they speak Zulu, but even between these two there are subtle differences. Kumalo's sentences are extremely simple and comprise a limited vocabulary, reflecting a language which despite its capacity to express feeling, contains a relatively small number of words. Kumalo's speech also reflects his ecclesiastical training, and makes frequent use of biblical phraseology and terms. Msimangu's speech is similar in these respects, but it is far more sophisticated, reflecting the fact that he lives in the cosmopolitan city of Johannesburg.

Native Speech

The extreme simplicity and rhythmic quality which characterize the conversation of Kumalo and Msimangu are also reflected in the conversations of most of the native people. The rhythmic quality of the native speech arises out of the repetition that primitive languages use to convey ideas. The limited vocabulary of such languages requires that ideas be defined by first approximating what the idea is, and then what the idea is not. For example, if the language does not contain both the words "meeting" and "accompanying," but only the words "come together," the idea of "accompanying" might be phrased "They came together. They did not come together. They did not come alone." Repetition is also made necessary by the limited **syntax** of such languages, which therefore requires repetition of the subject or subject idea.

Thus many of the shorter conversations between native characters have almost the quality of a small song, or the way such a song might sound in translation. Paton uses this pattern for brief conversations throughout the book with great effect. When he dramatizes the desperate housing problems of the native people in their segregated quarters, he creates the pattern deliberately in song forms. In some cases he uses a basic line which is repeated with alternate responses, and in some cases he uses alternate statements followed by a statement which is repeated like a refrain.

White Speech

The speech of Jarvis, his wife, and the other white people is totally different in the sense that the word order, phrasing, and use of constructions presents the familiar English that we know. But more than that, the language is less formal, more easy, as befits the language of those whose tongues are not constrained by translation and need for deference. For example, where a native woman would say, 'My husband, what is it?" a white woman would use her husband's name and say, "What's the matter?" This ease of language is even reflected in the decidedly deferential speech of white inferiors to their superiors in the book.

The differentiation of character through speech is most evident in the conversations between Jarvis and John Harrison, his daughter-in-law's brother. Jarvis, a quiet, reserved man who speaks little, utters mostly brief, simple statements which occasionally contain signs of the native influence. Harrison, on the other hand, is given to lengthy statements, characterized by the use of slang and cliches.

Speech and Attitude

The author also uses differences of tone to convey the attitudes and the fears which characterize the white people in Africa. In a series of passages which convey these aspects through a variety of anonymous white speakers, Paton presents us with several cogent examples which express various prevalent attitudes. These range from self-righteous indignation to well-meaning but pompous liberalism, and from an upholding of the status quo to a fearful desire to maintain social status. All of these speakers are only identified by what they say and how they say it, but they need no further description in this book.

Language as Point of View

As we noted earlier in this discussion, the author has made it possible for the reader to experience rather than merely to observe the story through his use of language, and there are two remaining techniques of this kind in the novel that should be noted. One should already have become evident from the discussion up to this point. This is the way that Paton enables us to observe action through the eyes of the observer, rather than in appropriate, objective terms. This technique is used with particular effectiveness when Paton uses native observers to describe engineering operations in the Umzimkulu. Through the eyes of the speaker, it is as if we were seeing these things for the first time.

Matter Quoted at Length

The other method we should note is the way the author employs prose sections which appear as matter quoted at length. For example, when Paton presents an incident in the form of a quoted newspaper story, we are made aware of how this incident, whose background we know, would appear to the world at large. Again, when Paton presents us with an essay or a legal document, we are presented with a theoretical and logical **exposition** of a situation we have seen only emotionally, in terms of action and character.

THE HUMAN LEVEL: CHARACTERS IN PARABLE

Like the language, the characters and settings of *Cry, the Beloved Country* appear in several aspects and perform several functions simultaneously. They are characters in a parable, they are unique individuals, they are embodiments of the political and social forces explored in the novel, and they are symbols of the human spirit choosing between fear and love. The parable in the novel can be interpreted in terms of the persons of Stephen Kumalo and James Jarvis, and their children and grandchildren, in the places of the mountains and basin of the Umzimkulu valley, and in Johannesburg. But the meaning of the parable lies in the ideas that these individuals stand for, and for that we must turn to the clues that the author has given us.

God and Satan

To begin with, James Jarvis appears to represent God Himself. He represents a kind of Jehovah who lives in a heaven, or paradise, far above those to whom his word is law. We can also determine that Stephen Kumalo is, in the parable a kind of Satan, the fallen angel, the Prince of Hell. But Paton does not use the image of Satan as a willful, evil spirit. Instead, it is Satan as that angel who was once the brightest star in heaven, rivaling even the brightness of God himself. When we consider the pious, loving, and profound Stephen Kumalo, this may seem strange, but there are good reasons for following this idea. Even as Satan was cast into hell by God after a fierce battle between the angels of darkness and light, so the black tribes of Africa were subjugated by the white man and "cast" into a small and lesser part of South Africa. There is a slightly devilish side to Kumalo too, for on several occasions his anger overcomes him and he torments those most dear to him even as he torments himself. This aspect of Kumalo certainly belongs more to a Satanic image than a priestly one. And of course, the first time that we see Kumalo step down from his saintly role, it is into the sin of pride, the sin for which Satan was cast out of heaven.

Arthur as Christ

The meaning of the parable continues in their sons, Arthur and Absalom. Arthur is certainly the most saintly character in the book, and in the parable, he represents Christ himself. First, he is the son of "God." Secondly, he left "heaven" to go into the world, which is, of course, Johannesburg. Thirdly, he has made an active decision to serve mankind, which is, in the novel, the people of South Africa. There is also his total devotion to good and, like Christ, he was no revolutionary, but in intent, at least, he was a reformer of the existing ethic, Christianity. Further, his death was brought about by one closest to him, a member of that native population with whose well-being he was most concerned.

Johannesburg, The World

Then let us look at the meaning of Johannesburg itself. It stands for the world and worldly things. It is the center of all human activity: a city dedicated to the god, Mammon, for it is the city of gold, being built both literally and figuratively on its gold mines. Thus it is not a city of God, but a sinful city divided against itself, echoing to some extent Sodom and Gomorrah. At the same time it is "a city of wonders," where side by side with greed and crime there is love and courage, lawlessness and justice mingled, just as they are in the world at large. In other words, Johannesburg can be saved, if it will listen to its men of God.

Absalom as Judas

And to the world of Johannesburg came another man, Absalom, the son of darkness, who succumbed to the corruption of the great city. Absalom's role in the parable is primarily that of

Judas. Like Judas, he betrays a man who wished nothing but his welfare for a paltry object - the equivalent of Judas' thirty pieces of silver. It should also be noted that Absalom is virtually the embodiment of that fear which Paton sees at the root of all men's troubles. He kills in fear, he responds with fear, and in the end, it is his fear that remains.

Something Bright

But the final threads of the parable lie in the children, principally in Arthur Jarvis' unnamed son. Here we have a modern Christchild par excellence. He is "otherworldly," seeming to be unaware that white children do not show deference to natives, even to native priests. He is "something bright," like a light in the darkness of the native world. He is also the son of Mary and is descended from God. But most important of all is the role of the boy in the story, for he becomes, like Christ, the intercessor between God and fallen man. It is "Christ" who brings the human condition to the attention of "God," and it is through his intercession that the prayers of the fallen angels are heard.

In essence then, the meaning of the parable is an enactment of Paton's thesis that only love can overcome the fear which is destroying Africa (and the world). The present situation has been created by the past. It is a situation where the white people (the conquerors) hold such power that they live like gods, while the native people (the conquered) live as outcasts in the land. Today this situation is no longer permissible, and thus breeds violence, which harms everyone. The solution lies in the future - in the children. But in the meantime, it is necessary for those in power to help those who have neither power or means to raise themselves to a level in which they can share in the bounty of the land (and the world).

CRY, THE BELOVED COUNTRY

CHARACTER ANALYSES

THE HUMAN LEVEL: CHARACTERS AS INDIVIDUALS

The individual characters of *Cry, the Beloved Country* are very substantially human and unique, but with the exception of Kumalo and Jarvis, their personalities are not fully revealed to us. The characters are realized as psychologically functioning individuals in varying degrees, to the extent that they represent types and ideals of South Africa. For example, some, like Gertrude and the young man who heads the boys' reformatory, are occasionally glimpsed as individuals, but often appear as types. On the other hand, some are seen solely as types. And in all cases, the personalities are so entwined with their political activities and concerns, as well as with the viewpoint they represent in the total outlook of the novel, that it is impossible to view them merely as human beings in a private moment in their lives. However, it is important to the appreciation of the novel to see the extent to which Paton has developed character as such, and we shall make an attempt to isolate this aspect for our analytic purposes.

Reverend Stephen Kumalo

One of the two fully realized characters is of course the Reverend Stephen Kumalo. We know nothing of his family or upbringing except that he is a Zulu and speaks that language. How he came to choose the ministry or how he was able to obtain an education is not told. But we do learn quickly that while he is very kind, he also has a cruel streak which is sometimes turned inward against himself and sometimes outward at others. His kindness is apparent from the first, while his capacity for sudden cruelty have been noted above. The reader learns that he is also timid, and on the whole passive, which often makes him appear childlike, a characteristic for which we see him try to compensate with an artificial pride. But against these weaknesses we are made aware of a fierce and genuine drive to do what is right and good and necessary and a great capacity for tenderness and understanding. Despite his own disabilities, we see him as a man who also has great insight into others although this insight is mostly confined to native people.

Kumalo also appears as a man who has a deep capacity for feeling, and much of the immediacy of the novel comes from the author's ability to express this fact. In contrast to the outward calm which characterizes Jarvis, Kumalo is a sensitive instrument, responding deeply and completely to the events and people that confront him. But this is not something which can easily be illustrated, for the author creates this sensibility from a thousand subtle words and actions. The combination of insight and determination which characterizes Kumalo also enable him to survive and to continue to struggle and even to gain in understanding.

James Jarvis, Esquire

The figure of James Jarvis, Esquire (as he is introduced), is Kumalo's antithesis in many ways. Where Kumalo is seen as timid, Jaris appears confident, sure of his position and the rightness of his actions. Where Kumalo is, in many ways a philosopher, Jarvis has rarely given much thought to political and philosophical matters. While we learn he is aware of the South African problem and the many approaches and objections to its solution, they appear to be catalogued in his mind, rather than considered as grounds for personal choice. In fact, we never find out what goes on within Jarvis's mind; we only know how he appears at various moments and what he says. And yet, he is substantial. Rather than being a man whose feelings we do not know, we recognize in him a person who has lived for so long in a safe, rarified world that he is unused to calling upon deep, violent emotions in relation to other people. He appears as a man who has loved his land, his wife, and his son, and whose only fierce feeling seems to have been his belief in individual independence, a conviction to which he held true even with respect to his own son.

Theophilus Msimangu

Msimangu is in many ways an idealized character, although the author has made him seem real to us. His kindness, his steadfastness, his sense of reality, his profound outlook on life, his insight, make him appear like an ideal Kumalo. Yet we become aware that his character is maintained only through a continuous inner struggle. Yet it is perhaps the extent of his struggle that makes him so "real" to us, so comprehensible despite the extent of his virtues.

John Kumalo

Another person whose struggle between his ideal and his reality is less successful is Kumalo's brother, John Kumalo. To a substantial degree, John Kumalo is more the personification of a type than an individual, but Paton has given him human dimension by letting us see the private motives that have brought him to his stand. He appears as a man deeply concerned with matters of money and status, and we learn that even in his political oratory, he speaks carefully so that he can maintain his status without losing his possessions. We recognize in him a firm believer in what would be called in America "the gimmick," the rest of whose faith lies in power. But it is not the power of love, for we are made aware that he is totally unscrupulous in acting for his own advantage.

Gertrude And Mrs. Lithebe

The characters of Mrs. Lithebe, Kumalo's devout landlady in Johannesburg, and of Gertrude, his sister, are in many ways, types. Viewed in this way, Mrs. Lithebe is the native who has come to terms with the white man on his terms, finding a pattern for her life in the ethics of her religion. She is kind and generous, but is strict in holding to the social and sexual behaviour permitted by her church. Gertrude, who is young enough to be Kumalo's daughter, is Mrs. Lithebe's antithesis. She cannot accept the terms of the old way of life but suffers under the deprivation which the new way entails. The pull between the desire for the security of the old native world and the freedom of the insecure life of the native in Johannesburg is expressed in the novel through her. Gertrude's choice appears to be a choice between sexual freedom and celibacy, but one suspects that the constraint of life under the old native forms involves more than that. However badly a native may have to live in the city, a person like Gertrude will at least avoid the constant call to a goodness she does not feel in herself that would confront her in a native town. Although she is a lesser character in the book, Gertrude's inner conflict and choice give her a depth which the more ethical and kind Mrs. Lithebe lacks.

The Girl

The young girl who is Absalom's common-law wife, is a frail, delicate character whose existence in the novel seems as tenuous as it is in her reality. But in part this is due to the fact that she represents not a type, but an idea. For she and her children represent the future of native South Africa. Her youth and her desire make her malleable, and in her eagerness to learn we can see a possibility for native adaptation to the future.

The Remaining Characters

Father Vincent represents in part those white men in the church who are concerned with the welfare of the natives, and on the whole, he fulfills this function gracefully. Napoleon Letsitsi, the young native demonstrator, and John Harrison, represent roles rather than individuals, and will be shown in this aspect below. There are also the unnamed children: Gertrude's child, Arthur Jarvis's son, and the unborn child of Absalom, who are all embodiments of what Paton sees as South Africa's hope; they are all the children of South Africa.

THE POLITICAL LEVEL: MEN, SOCIETY AND ECONOMICS

Cry, the Beloved Country is not a story of people only; it is also a political pamphlet. In the words and the lives of the characters as well as in expository passages, Paton states a carefully thoughtout body of ideas which are concerned with the causes of the South African dilemma, the reasons for its continued existence, the dangers of the situation, and approaches to its solution. While he presents many viewpoints on these aspects of the problem, it is clear that he believes only one is feasible, and to a great extent, the novel's third book is an **exposition** of the way that Paton believes will work.

The Situation

The fundamental political problem of South Africa is that one-fifth of the population owns ninety percent of the land, controls virtually all the means of production, and holds a similar portion of its wealth. This minority is white, holds political power, and is enfranchised. Four-fifths of the population are kept in compounds or especially designated city districts which include the remaining one-tenth of the land, control virtually none of its production, and hold but a small fraction of its wealth. This four-fifths is black, colored (of mixed race), and Indian, holds no legitimate power, and is disenfranchised. One does not need more than this meager picture of the approximate statistics to understand the nature of the South African situation.

The Causes

The causes of the dilemma lie partly in the history of the country. This includes the development of resources with unskilled labor; the setting up of laborers' compounds to separate the women and children from the harsh social and economic life of the mining towns; the failure to provide for native education; the destruction of a tribal system that impeded the growth of the country; and the subsequent attempt to preserve the tribal system, as a means of preserving order, by a policy of segregation.

There are, however, corresponding causes in the present. The unskilled labor is kept unskilled to ensure its availability as such. The setting up of compounds has destroyed native family life and put nothing in its place. Despite the fact that native education is now necessary to enable native children to develop socially desirable attitudes, the white elements have not provided adequate native educational facilities. The tribal system has not been replaced by any other native social order. And the segregation policy has been unfairly administered: the disproportionately small amount of land given to the native population has forced the immigration of labor into the towns, creating the slums and crime which the white community now bewails.

Peonage and Status Quo

The reason for the continued existence of this situation can be summarized in one word: peonage, a servitude little better than slavery. The white minority feels completely dependent for its wealth on the cheap labor provided by the native population, and wants to ensure that it will stay cheap. This is expressed again and again throughout the novel by people who stand on very different sides. The people who stand on the side of integration, or at least economic equality, point out that when a new source of gold is found or production is increased, the increase in income is not used to increase native laborer's wages but to increase the already substantial wealth of the white owners. The people who stand on the side of the status quo, on the other hand, insist that an increase in native wages would make operation of the mines uneconomical. Since these people see the South African economy as built on its mines, they presume that an increase in the native labor share of the wealth would result in economic disaster.

Dangers and Solutions

As to the dangers, there is, of course, the danger of the violence which would follow a united native uprising. Another, which would follow an uprising or a native general strike, is the danger that the industry of South Africa, the industry on which South Africa depends, would come to a standstill, bringing economic disaster. Still another danger is self-enclosure of the white South African population in a state of fear.

But as to what should be done, there are a thousand answers current in South Africa, and Paton presents several of these through the voices of anonymous commentators. But to Paton it is obvious that the broad outlines of the solution are clear. The white man must help the native. At the outset this help will have to be paternalistic in nature. The white man must use his money, his knowledge, and his technology to determine what must be done and see that it is done. But at the same time, it is vital that the natives cooperate in the process, and that gifted individuals among them be educated immediately to help in this reclamation. The reader gathers that Paton considers the white man's responsibility for improvement of native conditions to be justified as a form of restitution of what he has previously confiscated and reformation of a situation he himself has created.

The Philosophy: Love

The basic philosophical premise on which *Cry, the Beloved Country* proceeds is that the troubles of South Africa, like the troubles of mankind, arise out of man's fear, and that this fear can only be cast out by love. Paton points out that the disparity between the ideal and the reality is created because man is afraid: of losing his identity, if he truly acts on the idea of the brotherhood of man; and of losing his possessions, if he acknowledges that all are entitled to the use of their diverse gifts. The antagonism between black and white is thus based on fear. While there is no ultimate political solution to South Africa's (and the world's) problems, there is an ultimate solution in Paton's philosophy. That philosophy holds that salvation can only come when man overcomes his fear by love.

This thesis is demonstrated throughout the entire novel. Those who act out of fear have no room in their hearts for love. Therefore they cannot help to alleviate the problem which impinges on their lives; they can only accentuate it. But for those for whom love is their motive power, the fear that rises in their hearts is struggled with and overcome, sometimes by their love of others, and sometimes by the love of others for them. But what Paton means by love is something greater than personal or paternal affection. Its meaning lies closer to compassion, an objective love that has no hint of pity.

Vocabulary

Assessors are advisors to a judge in South Africa.

Die spoor loop dood means "The trail runs dead" in Afrikaans.

Donga is a bank or steep side of a river.

Inkosana means "little master' or "little chief" in Zulu.

Inkosi means "master" or "chief" in Zulu.

Inkosikazi means "Madame" or "Mrs." in Zulu.

Jy is 'n goeie Kaffer means "You are a good Kaffir" in Afrikaans.

Judge is used in South Africa only when referring to a Supreme Court justice.

Kafferboetie means "little brother" in Afrikaans, but it is used as an insulting term by most whites in South Africa. The American equivalent would be "nigger lover."

Kaffir means "African native," but it is an insulting word.

Kloof is a ravine or ditch dug in the earth by the rain.

Lobola is the custom of buying a wife with cattle.

Magistrate is an ordinary judge.

Maize means "corn."

Mealies are ears of corn.

Nkosi sikelel' iAfrika means "God Save Africa." It is the name of a song used by native Africans as their national anthem.

Pro deo means "for God" in Latin.

Siyafa means "we die."

Tixo means "God" in Xosa.

Umfundisi means "parson" in Zulu.

Umnumzana means "sir" in Zulu.

Umzimkulu means "great river" in Zulu, but the river by that name is really small.

USmith means "Mr. Smith" in Zulu.

Veld means "prairie" and is pronounced like "felt." It is an Afrikaans word but is used also in English.

CRY, THE BELOVED COUNTRY

REVIEW OF CRITICISM

Paton has been praised highly for his sociological study of racial conditions in South Africa and for his humanitarian efforts on behalf of non-Europeans there. He has also been recognized to some extent as a "religious" writer. Although it was generally well received, there is some difference of opinion as to the literary merits of *Cry, the Beloved Country*. For the most part, critics have been pleased by Paton's use of language, by his sympathetic characterizations, and by the poetic quality of his novel. There is less agreement on the effectiveness and meaning of the symbols in the novel.

PATON AS A SOCIOLOGICAL NOVELIST

Adrienne Koch, in a review of the novel published in the *Saturday Review of Literature*, calls Paton both a "social scientist" and a highly serious novelist. Paton's novel is based on a long study of social conditions in South Africa. The Rev. Trevor Huddleston, C.R., an English priest who has worked for many years in the African slums of Johannesburg, says that Paton has very clearly described the atmosphere of those slums in this novel. Harold R.

Collins, in an article in *College English*, states that anthropological studies confirm both Paton's description of life in the slums of Johannesburg and his description of the decay of the tribe and tribal morality. Collins finds that both Absalom and his girl represent the condition of African morality. The African religion has been destroyed for them, even though they retain some superstitions, and they have not fully accepted Christianity. Even though this may be the usual condition, Paton does not appear to be saying that Christianity means nothing to Absalom. He did come from a thoroughly Christian home. His Christian morality is corrupted, however, in the slums of Johannesburg. It is true that the values of the Church, in which both Absalom and his girl were supposedly reared, meant little to them until the Rev. Stephen Kumalo arrived in Johannesburg. When faced with his crimes, Absalom is filled with a sense of guilt based on Christian morality and his father's presence makes him greatly ashamed. He had given in to pagan superstition when he accepted without objection the blessing by a witchdoctor of Pafuri's iron bar.

PATON AS A RELIGIOUS WRITER

Paton indirectly confirms the opinion that *Cry, the Beloved Country* is a sociological novel, but he also indicates that he writes from a religious viewpoint. In a paper on "The South African Novel in English," Paton says that the South African writing in English "turns to race as his main **theme**" and to "the drama and conflict that is bound up with race." "I myself," he writes, "have a religious view of the universe." Charles J. Rolo, in the *Atlantic Monthly*, says that the "mainspring of this unusual book is saintliness." Not only are a number of important characters in the novel priests of the Church of England, but both Arthur Jarvis and Stephen Kumalo are saintly, and the novel preaches Christian love.

The Rev. Stephen Kumalo is the chief figure in the novel and it is his love for his family that drives him to Johannesburg. He is helped there by the Rev. Theophilus Msimangu and Father Vincent. Msimangu says that John Kumalo has been corrupted because he does not understand love. Only love cannot be corrupted. Arthur Jarvis, whose writings reflect the views of Alan Paton, believes that only love can save South Africa. Love and saintliness are the same in this novel.

The religious view is essentially a mystical one. Kumalo learns more about the corruption of men in South Africa, but he learns to accept the mystery of pain and suffering. There is no explanation for suffering, but Kumalo learns to accept it because of the love he experiences and because of his faith. This religious point of view applies even to the soil. The land around High Place, the farm of James Jarvis, is holy or sacred because men have guarded or kept it just as it came from God. Napoleon Letsitsi is called an angel of God for the simple reason that he has come to restore this land. Paton, therefore, sees the work of this agricultural demonstrator from a religious as well as a sociological point of view. Because of his part in establishing a chain of events which bring about the restoration of the land, the son of Arthur Jarvis is also called an angel or messenger of God.

PATON'S UTOPIAN DREAM

In the third section of the novel, Paton does not write as a social scientist who describes what really exists. He writes primarily as a man who dreams of what may be. Stephen Kumalo's spiritual development is credible because he grows stronger and learns to love more when he faces the bitter truth about his tribe and his son's fate. The comfort that comes to him from Jarvis and Letsitsi is less believable. It is, as Charles J. Rolo has said, "unfortunately a trifle pat: milk for the sick child, a new church, a dam for the stricken valley."

The third section of the novel also changes the nature of Paton's novel. The death of Arthur Jarvis, the execution of Absalom, the broken heart of Stephen Kumalo are all caused by forces outside their control. Their downfall is, in other words, tragic. The third section of the novel gives the book a happy and hopeful ending. Paton has carefully constructed a chain of events that lead to the work of restoration of the valley. It begins with Arthur Jarvis.

Unfortunately Arthur Jarvis is a shadowy person even though his opinions are very clear. He has no human failings or peculiar habits. He is believable only because he does not appear and is described by others or revealed by his writings. Kumalo is credible because he has faults and because we see him in contact with others. The first two parts of the novel describe a world in which greed, hate, fear, and ignorance are almost everywhere. Suddenly, because of the influence of an almost divine person, Arthur Jarvis, love conquers all these with ease and gives promise of a better world. Arthur Jarvis really serves, in this last section, as a **deus ex machina**, or an improbable or unexpected solution to the central problem of the novel, the destruction of the tribe and tribal land.

CHARACTERIZATION

In spite of this flaw, *Cry, the Beloved Country* is still a good novel. This is largely due to Paton's sympathetic portrayal of characters like Kumalo, Absalom's girl, and James Jarvis. Kumalo's slowness, his ignorance of city life, his quick temper, and a desire to hurt others when angry make his virtues appear all the more real.

Absalom's girl engages the sympathy of the reader because, in spite of her shadowy personality, she appears as a lonely little girl who suddenly responds to the affection given her by the Kumalos.

STYLE AND SYMBOLISM

M. C. Hubbard, in the *New York Herald Tribune Weekly Book Review*, praises this novel for its fine prose style, but Paton's use of symbols is not liked by everyone. Paton uses cadenced language that reminds one of the prose of the King James' version of the Bible. He also uses effectively idioms that are peculiar to Zulu. Charles Rolo finds that the symbolism of the final pages of the novel is a failure. He is, of course, referring to the breakfast and dawn following a night of prayer on the mountain. This breakfast of corn bread and tea is described in biblical language that reminds one of the Anglican Communion Service. Paton's purpose seems to be to indicate that Kumalo now fully understands love and suffering and is united with God. He has learned to accept pain and suffering just as Christ accepted them. The exact meaning of the breakfast as a symbol is not clear. The dawn is perhaps too clear a symbol of the hopefulness of the future. Sheridan Baker, in an article in *College English*, finds that geographical symbolism unifies the whole novel. In brief, mountains symbolize moral superiority and plains (or valleys) symbolize whatever is corrupt. Even though Johannesburg is actually higher than Ndotsheni, it is thought of as the corrupt city of the plain according to Mr. Baker.

STRUCTURE

These mountains and the forlorn crying of the titihoya are symbols related to the careful parallel structure of the novel.

The ground of High Place, the James Jarvis farm in the uplands, is holy and good things come from it. Kumalo prays to God on the mountains. Johannesburg is the corrupt city in the plain where Kumalo is tested and made strong. The titihoya appears at the beginning, middle, and end of the novel. It calls upon the people of Africa to turn from hate and fear to love. One father, James Jarvis, lives in the mountains where the titihoya cries. The other, Kumalo, lives in the desolate valley where the titihoya no longer cries. Each one goes to Johannesburg, the city of the plain, to find his son. One son has murdered the other and the murderer is to be executed. Both fathers learn more about Africa as a result of their experience in Johannesburg. They learn to overcome racial prejudice which has kept them apart for years. The novel ends on a note of hope for the Africa of their grandsons.

CRY, THE BELOVED COUNTRY

ESSAY QUESTIONS AND ANSWERS

Question: What is the central **theme** of *Cry, the Beloved Country*?

Answer: The central **theme** is love. This means love for all people and for the land. Love is possible only when one conquers his fears and his greed. This love, however, requires that the individual first learn to understand the nature and causes of fear in others.

Question: Why is *Cry, the Beloved Country* a propaganda novel?

Answer: Because it is Paton's intention to show that apartheid, or the policy of racial segregation, is morally and socially evil. The lives of two young men are taken primarily because of this evil. Paton describes the extreme misery, poverty and humiliation which are the results of this policy. Good houses and doctors, because of apartheid, are available only to whites. It is also very difficult for Africans to lead moral lives. This is because they are forced to live in crowded slums which encourages crime and discourages responsible relationships between people. Thus slums destroy both families and individuals.

Question: Why cannot the whites solve the racial problem justly?

Answer: It is because they are greedy and fearful. The whites are filled with fear of attack which keeps them from examining objectively the cause of native crime. Those who control the wealth of the country are fearful because they might lose part of their profits if Africans were able to insist on decent wages. Yet, it is this very fear and greed which crowds the Africans into slums and isolates husbands from their wives in compounds which break up family life and morality. Morality is destroyed when the family is broken up, and crime increases with the loss of morality.

Question: Why cannot total apartheid work?

Answer: Apartheid cannot work because the areas assigned to the native Africans cannot support them and because they are needed in mining, industry, and agriculture in the white areas to support the white economy. Sixty five percent of the people of South Africa are Africans and yet they own only sixteen percent of the land. A good part of their land is too dry for extensive farming and African farmers usually use old-fashioned methods of farming which ruin the land. This poorly farmed and dry land cannot support the Africans living on the native reserves and the growing population must go elsewhere. Many leave to work in the cities, in the mines, and on the farms and citrus ranches of the white farmers. In theory these African workers are only temporary residents of the areas outside the native reserves. However, if all Africans were to leave the mines, factories, and white farms, South African economy would come to a halt. As a matter of fact, in spite of apartheid, Africans in increasing numbers are leaving the native reserves.

INTRODUCTION TO TOO LATE THE PHALAROPE

....

The novel, *Too Late the Phalarope*, is a pessimistic-even perhaps a despairing-book. The symbol of the phalarope is deeply imbedded in the meaning of the story itself, and the precise delineation of its significance is a matter for conjecture. But this much is certain-it is a bird which is indigenous to all parts of South Africa and as such probably represents its spirit, and a basis for an understanding between men. But in the novel its recognition and the understanding it brings come too late to save the country.

The novel is a beautifully written, tightly constructed, deeply felt work, which is profound in its content and thus may be subject to several kinds of interpretation. For our purposes it will be useful to view it as a psychological parable, for, as such, we can examine the story, the action, and the characters from a single, all-inclusive point of view. Using this interpretation, the hero, Pieter van Vlaanderen, represents all of South Africa; and his environment, the town and people of Venterspan, represent all the forces in the Country, which have created all that is best and worst in it and will finally destroy the best and the worst together.

Before we determine precisely how this parable functions in the novel, it is necessary to know what these forces are, their source in the history and religion of South Africa, and how they operate in South Africa today.

THE FORCES AND THEIR ORIGINS

The forces are fear, pride, hate, distrust, rigidity, and Puritanism. In part they have been nurtured in the Afrikan people by their history. Having taken the coastal land once by the courage and determination of the first Dutch settlers, they found themselves displaced by the British. Moving inland, they took the land again-by force from the native warrior tribes of the interior-only to find themselves again in conflict with the British over the gold and diamond wealth which was centered in the interior city of Johannesburg. After the long and bitter struggle of the Boer War they took the land again from the British, but it was through a postwar settlement, for they had lost the war. Alan Paton summed up the consequences himself in a speech made in 1949: "The Afrikaner still feared that he and his world would be swallowed up and lost in the great British culture. He also saw a danger that the traditional English policy of laissez faire toward the black people might lead to his engulfment." So the Afrikaner was determined to re-establish his original distinctness and return to his original policy of "survival and separation." Thus we can see the sources of the Afrikaner's fear and pride-pride in his accomplishments and his identification with them, and fear of losing that identification by absorption into the rest of the world. But in South Africa, as in the rest of humanity, the consequence of fear is hate and distrust.

In part the forces ambient in South Africa today have also been created by their religion and its moral code, which is based on the Protestant ethic. This ethic has also played a large and many-sided role in the development of the American personality; but while it was softened by the influence of the many cultures which form the American people, it was made harsher by the harshness of Afrikaner history and by the militant posture they assumed in their defense. Today this ethic is directly manifest in the Afrikan society's demands for absolute obedience-to duty and authority and to the requirements of Puritan morality. Nor in the ethic removed from its religious origins. It is learned and practiced in terms of a religious idea which is substantially fundamentalist, taking its impetus directly from the Bible. As with all tradition-directed societies geared to the Protestant ethic, Afrikan society is also patriarchal, a characteristic which has been emphasized by its history. Finally, the society is characterized by an especially sharp distinction between the life roles of men and women, which, like the patriarchal structure, was inherent in the religion of Luther and was made sharper by historical necessity.

THE BACKGROUND OF THE HERO

With this background we can approach *Too Late the Phalarope* in term of the parents of the hero, Jakob and Mina van Vlaanderen. They represent a fairly typical Afrikan family whose character is entirely determined by the societal pattern we have outlined above. The father of such a family rules it in a tradition-oriented, patriarchal fashion, demanding absolute obedience and observance of duty, and behavior which is appropriate to the family member's sexual role. He is also a strong man whose determination and strength has enabled him to achieve great personal success at the price of great personal rigidity. He has a fixed outlook on the relationship of God and man; on the role of man in the world; and on the duty of man and woman in terms of the Protestant ethic. The mother in such a family is totally subservient to the father, but second to him in power and importance. But while she is able to demand obedience from the rest of the family in her own right, she does so traditionally out of gentleness, which, like the more delicate human attributes of expressiveness and sensitivity, is her domain. However, she must, like her husband, obey and express the highly restrictive moral ethic of the society, and particularly those more concerned with sexual expression.

Now we can see some of the inner forces which drive the hero, Pieter. Since the father and mother represent the models for the standard by which the son judges himself and others in the world, the son is forced to view only his aggressive, competitive, and logical approaches to life as masculine and therefore desirable in himself, and his receptive, non-competitive, and intuitive approaches to life as feminine, and therefore undesirable in himself. At the same time he is required to exercise constant self-control to be obedient, dutiful, and otherwise well-behaved in accordance with the Protestant ethic and repress all traces of feelings and behavior which do not accord with its ideal. To some extent, these requirements also exist in the American family and society, but they are held to with far less rigidity, permitting considerable latitude for the expression of individual differences. This latitude is almost completely lacking in the Afrikan society.

Since the masculine ideal of the Afrikan society is thus based entirely on a personality ordered solely by an individual's consciousness, his unconscious feelings - those which can find no outlet because they are undesirable - are almost totally repressed. They are only permitted to appear in certain highly restricted ways, such as the telling of dirty jokes, which must be confined to masculine company of a certain age range.

However, to the best of our psychological knowledge to date, the subconscious is by far the "largest" part of the individual, being the source and reservoir of all his life energy; of all his important ideas, understandings, and attitudes; and of his strongest feelings and basic motivations-desirable or undesirable. We also understand that if the aspects which are considered undesirable in an individual are not acknowledged and dealt with in an acceptable manner, in the light of day - i.e.: by his consciousness - their power within him will drive him to express them compulsively - in some form which is beyond his control. And this is what happened to Pieter van Vlaanderen.

THE HERO AS SOUTH AFRICA

In the parable of *Too Late the Phalarope*, Pieter represents the entire South African society, white and black. On the one hand, he is a man who is the embodiment of its highest ethic, which includes all the capacities and virtues which the white society strives for and sees itself as having. He also represents all the economic and social advantages of the white society as well as its governmental power, which in South Africa has become something like police activity. On the other hand, he contains in himself a powerful, forcibly repressed urge which represents all that the white society fears and has attributed to its native population: uncontrolled emotions and feelings-a compound of hate, anger, and sexual desire, and indirectly, a wish to destroy the source of its frustration: that is, the white society. This urge is compressed into a single compulsive lust for what it sees as the embodiment of itself-its proper mate-a native.

Thus the hero represents both the white, ethically-controlled society and the larger repressed native population, a land that is, like the hero, divided against itself. Like the hero, the South

African society attempts to control itself by complete repression of white unconscious feelings and black people. At the same time, like the hero, it also engages in desperate attempts to handle its situation through its church, its white minorities, its authorities, and its women. (The last are active in various societies throughout the Country.) But the church, personified in the novel by the young dominee, is too identified with the white national ideal to perceive that anything is wrong with the status quo. The white minorities, who are less identified with the ideal and can see the situation more objectively, are personified by Abraham Kaplan. But although they are aware of the problem, they are too conscious of their borderline status in an intolerant society to dare to assert themselves as equals, which they must do before they can help. The authorities, personified by Captain Jooste, are too involved in maintaining their paternal role and the rigid standards of duty until it is too late. And the women, personified by Nella van Vlaanderer, are too afraid and repressed to see the situation for what it really is and are therefore also incapable of helping South Africa in time.

PHALAROPES AND STAMPS

The parable also represents the idea that the old self-sufficient South Africa, represented by Jakob, and the new self-divided South Africa, represented by Pieter, might have come to an understanding after all by a common bond through which they can be united - the love of South Africa and its spirit, the phalarope itself. But by the time that bond is recognized, the novel implies, it will be too late.

This **theme** is emphasized in the novel through the symbol of the stamps. The stamps can be viewed as representing people; like people, Paton implies, they are worth more together than the sum of their separate values. They also represent people from divergent backgrounds, for the valued stamps are gathered from all parts of South Africa. Thus the love of stamps represents the humanitarian impulse which is frustrated in the novel by the old Nationalist Afrikaners in the person of Jakob. Again the novel implies that by the time the humanitarian ideal - the value of the stamps-can even be grudgingly recognized by the old order, it will be too late.

The structure of the novel is related to that of Greek tragedy, with "chorus," action and soliloquy alternating among each other. The chorus would be provided by Sophie van Vlaanderer when she speaks in her own person, while the soliloquies are of course the account of Pieter himself. It is possible that the novel may also contain echoes of Sophocles' *Oedipus*. Aside from the obvious parallels of the story (Oedipus kills his father unwittingly and is himself brought low, together with his children), there are several correspondences between Sophie as Tiresias, the blind, hermaphrodite seer. Both Sophie and Tiresias are, in a sense, outsiders, and see more than they wish to see, and both, in a sense, foresee the doom of the hero. As Tiresias says: "Unknowing you are enemy to kith and kin in death, beneath the earth and in this life. A deadly footed double striking curse, from (your) father . . . shall drive you forth out of this land, with darkness on your eyes, that now have such straight vision." So might Sophie have spoken.

TOO LATE THE PHALAROPE

REVIEW OF CRITICISM

A large number of critics have found that *Too Late the Phalarope* is even better than *Cry, the Beloved Country*. It is praised for its sympathetic characterizations and its fine language. Gilbert Highet called it a "superb novel" and said that Paton should in a few years get a Nobel Prize. The structure of this novel is tighter than that of his first one.

In this novel Paton gives sympathetic portraits, but he lays more stress on the conflict between characters, between natures, and between values. There is a conflict between chastity and sensuality, between love and harshness, between the Afrikaner and the Englishman, between two different notions of the nature of love. There are important struggles with the individual also. The van Vlaanderen family, says Edward Weeks in the *Atlantic Monthly*, appear to be "stern, proud, and pious," but behind this mask they are "at war with themselves." Jakob had a strong desire to hurt his son and an equally strong desire to win his affection. Pieter wants to confess or talk about his temptation or crime and yet resists efforts on the part of others to get him to talk freely with them.

One of the chief virtues of this book is, as Edward Weeks indicates, its "discernment of human motives." *Cry, the Beloved Country* is largely a sociological novel. This is primarily a psychological novel, or a novel in which the motives, feelings, and circumstances that influence action are examined. Pieter and Tante Sophie's behavior and feelings are examined in this way. He has a desire for love and also an equally strong desire to avoid love as not to be hurt. These two desires influence his behavior and bring about his tragic end. His aunt is a lonely woman who is denied love and children because of a facial disfigurement. She, therefore, treats Pieter the way she would her own son. She is fortunate in having a sister-in-law who is not jealous of her, but her nephew often hurts her when she tries to win his affections. It is because of her experience with Pieter's cruel words that she does not force him to speak about the problem. If he had he might have been saved.

The language of this novel is often biblical in its rhythms. This gives it a solemn, but somewhat monotonous, tone. The frequent use of Afrikaans words and expressions gives some color to the style.

Unlike *Cry, the Beloved Country*, this novel has a single plot, no digressions, and it is limited to one small geographical area. This is the story of Pieter van Vlaanderen, and everything related in the novel is directly related to his story. The story takes place in the country town of Venterspan and the region about it.

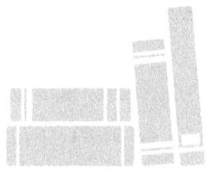

TOO LATE THE PHALAROPE

ESSAY QUESTIONS AND ANSWERS

Question: What are the racial and cultural conflicts in this novel?

Answer: There are two basic conflicts. The Afrikaners have strong feelings against both the English-speaking South Africans and against the African natives. Jakob van Vlaanderen and Sergeant Steyn represent those narrow Afrikaner nationalists who turned against Smuts when he supported England in the First World War. They support the Afrikaner language, their religion, and the white race, but they are opposed to England. Pieter is disowned by his father for fighting for England in the Second World War and Sergeant Steyn dislikes Pieter for the same reason. The magistrate and some of the women of Venterspan and Japie especially are concerned with the welfare of the Africans, but the general feeling towards them is harsh. They must use back doors, must not travel without a pass from the police, and physical contact with them is thought to be disgusting.

Question: In what sense is this novel a tragedy of sex?

Answer: Pieter van Vlaanderen and his wife Nella have entirely different attitudes towards sex. She is innocent and not very passionate even though she loves her husband. She thinks of sex as a minor part of marriage which is to be fitted into a fixed schedule of daily living. Pieter, on the other hand, requires not only the physical release of sex, but also the emotional passion that goes with it. Because his quiet little wife will not give this to him he turns to Stephanie, who is not at all ashamed of sex. Because of this his life and the lives of his wife and his family are ruined.

A TROUBLED LAND

INTRODUCTION

One might assume from a knowledge of Paton's work and the title that the ten stories, *Tales of a Troubled Land*, will be ten variations on the **theme** of apartheid in South Africa. But this is not the case, for both the stories of "The Worst Thing in His Life" and "The Elephant Shooter" are concerned with the behavior of people which does not have anything to do with apartheid per se. In fact, only the four stories which do not deal with Paton's experiences as principal of a native boys' reformatory - "Life for a Life," "The Waste Land," "Debbie Go Home," and "A Drink in the Passage" - are concerned with it immediately, and even "The Waste Land" deals with apartheid only symbolically. If we look further for a unifying or inclusive **theme**, we are also faced with the fact that such a story as "Ha'penny" could be told by the administrator of any institution for young delinquent boys. And in fact, each story could have taken place elsewhere; even the stories dealing directly with apartheid could have taken place in the American deep South. But while any one of these stories alone are not solely South African in content (except, perhaps, "The Elephant Shooter"), no other country can provide the background in which all ten could be placed together.

"LIFE FOR A LIFE"

No other country which could form the setting for the circumstances and the individuals of the other nine stories also manifests the particular evils we are forced to witness in the story of "Life for a Life." The first story of the book is written - and must be read - with a feeling of unmitigated fury, a fury which stands in stark contrast to the tone of the other stories in the book, even as violent and terrible a story as "The Waste Land." The tone of Paton's work generally (as we have noted earlier) is one of compassion and understanding, even of those who commit violent and terrible acts. But in "Life for a Life," the author presents us with a story in which the villain (for want of a better word) is not an individual or a type but the personification of a part of a society gone mad. There is no question, course, that individuals like Robbertse do exist-even as policemen. But such individuals are only permitted to act in an official capacity by the tacit if not the expressed approval of a society that desires the particular "services" they provide. The title of the story is vividly expressive of its theme-it is "Life for a Life," not "A Life for a Life." We must conclude, since Paton is a skilled craftsman, that the use of the general instead of a particular noun is deliberate. Therefore, the **theme** of the story is that the killing of Enoch Maarman by Robbertse represents deliberate murder - and especially murder of an innocent man - by a society, and that this is the most terrible act of all. This assumption does not in any way presume that Paton holds that the murder of one man by another is in any way justifiable. But it does imply that Paton views societal murder (as opposed to societal punishment by due process) as the destruction of life itself. For a man (and a society) whose profound religious convictions abhor the taking of a life as the worst crime a man can commit, the taking of an innocent life by common consent without law is the most terrible crime of all.

"THE WASTE LAND"

"Life for a Life" takes place in the environment of the Afrikaner farm where the present South African situation was born. In "The Waste Land," we are taken to the other "end" of that situation, for the setting of the story embodies all that is worst in the black environment that the white society has created through its policy of segregation. In this story Paton sketches, in a few brief and terrible strokes, the darkness of that Armageddon where the son raises his hand against the father, and the father brings down the son. In this story he also implies that the church, which should be man's refuge in the darkness, is separated from him as by a high wall, and his only access in his time of need is barred in such a way that it cannot be opened in time. "Death of a Tsotsi," reflects a similar **theme** - that isolated individual efforts, no matter how dedicated, cannot save those whom society has condemned to live in a wasteland from death as long as that society remains unchanged.

THREE BOYS AND THREE STORIES

The book contains three stories, "Sponono," "Ha'penny," and "The Divided House," which present us with three other victims of the South African condition, and three ways in which its victims attempt-unsuccessfully-to deal with their situation. The stories actually present very real and individual portraits of three boys whom Paton tried to help in his reformatory-portraits which Paton's brilliance as a writer raises to the level of art. In the larger context of the book, however, we can view these characters as typical. Thus Sponono represents the individual who has taken the white man at his word and accepts the white man's paternal role, and his own role as a willing but willful and dependent child, literally. There is much humor in the exchanges between Paton and Sponono, but the story, like the other two, is sad. Ha'penny's tragic story represents the failure to make life bearable through fantasy in the pitiless wasteland which makes its children homeless. In "The Divided House," Jacky epitomizes the native who struggles against odds which are too great for even the most ardent desire for the good life, symbolized by the idea of priesthood. Since the person of Jacky is the embodiment of both the desire for good and the forces against it-symbolized by the native South African narcotic weed, dagga-he also symbolizes the divided house of South Africa itself: the disparity between the ideal demanded by its Calvinist church and the dark reality dictated by its fears.

ASPECTS OF CHARACTER

There is an intermediate and less defined ground in the book which deals with aspects of the South African character. These aspects are covered by two stories: "The Worst Thing in His Life" and "The Elephant Shooter." In the first, we deal, among other things, with the disparity between the South African paternalistic ideal, represented in the story by both Paton and Jonkers, and the reality, which is their simple, human, economic concerns in the face of disaster. In the story, Paton represents himself with great humility as both the representative of governmental authority and as the same human being who is concerned with his career when he should be concerned with other matters. Jonkers represents the dutiful father, a pillar of his church, whose first thought in the face of a family disaster is for his job. In the story Paton considers the mockery of making Gods out of men, and demonstrates their feet of clay, not excluding his own.

In "The Elephant Shooter" we have perhaps the most hopeful story in the book, for Richard Coetzee seems to represent much that is both good and indigenous to South Africa. In him Paton has created a type of original man from the wilds of the country who is at once willful and constructive. The story can also be viewed as a parable of original man as the hunter who has respect for life, and goes out to bag bigger game which will nourish his people to health. The meaning of the parable lies in the idea that if the South African spirit can be directed toward constructive aims instead of killing, it will even be able to make pawns of the existing order for its ends.

COLORED, WHITE, AND BLACK

In the remaining two stories Paton shows us the actual workings of apartheid in two situations. In "Debbie Go Home" we see the position of South Africa's colored people-people of mixed racial background whose ancestors intermarried at a time when interracial marriages were still possible. Although they were not accepted by the Afrikaners, such people had, until recently, a wide range of personal and social freedom and some measure of power. With the fall of the Smuts Government and the assumption of power by the Afrikan Nationalists, the colored people have been reduced to native status. However, their background has made them far more constructively aggressive and individualistic than the native people. The story shows us how these people are torn by the ironic interaction between their fears and their personal, individual needs, and their awareness of the necessity for protest.

In "A Drink in the Passage" Paton presents us with the other side of the coin of apartheid - the distress of the liberal white society, and perhaps all that is liberal in South Africa. This element admires and even longs for a kind of communion with all that is best in native South Africa, personified by Edward

Simelane. Yet their fear prevents them from inviting the native completely into the house of their heart, so that they leave him standing at the door, where he is more exposed to danger than he is among his own people. The behavior of the people in the story thus represents the ineffectual and ambivalent efforts of the liberal whites. Their protests attract the attention of the Government but because they lack power, their protests often result in more repressive measures rather than in alleviation of the native condition. The future, Paton implies, remains in doubt.

BIBLIOGRAPHY

ABOUT SOUTH AFRICA

Huddleston, Trevor. *Naught for Your Comfort*. Garden City, N.Y.: Doubleday & Company, Inc., 1956.

Paton, Alan. *The Land and People of South Africa*. Philadelphia and New York: J. B. Lippincott Company, 1955.

Paton, Alan. *Hope for South Africa*. New York: Frederick A. Praeger, 1960.

Van Rensburg, Patrick. *Guilty Land: The History of Apartheid*. New York: Frederick A. Praeger, 1962.

CRY, THE BELOVED COUNTRY

Baker, Sheridan. "Paton's Beloved Country and the Morality of Geography," *College English*, XIX (October 1957), 56-61.

Collins, Harold R. "*Cry, the Beloved Country* and the Broken Tribe," *College English*, XIV (April 1953), 379-385.

Hubbard, M. C. *New York Herald Tribune Weekly Book Review,* February 1, 1948.

Kirkpatrick, Forrest H. *The Christian Century*, LXV (July 7, 1948), 684.

Koch, Adrienne. *Saturday Review of Literature*, XXXI (February 14, 1948), 14.

Sullivan, Richard. *New York Times*, February 1, 1948.

TOO LATE THE PHALAROPE

Highet, Gilbert. *Harper's Magazine*, CCVII (September 1953), 94.

Weeks, Edward. *Atlantic Monthly*, CLXXXII (September 1953), 70.

TALES FROM A TROUBLED LAND

Grunwald, Beverly. *Saturday Review of Literature*, XLIV (June 10, 1961), 25.

www.ingramcontent.com/pod-product-compliance
Lightning Source LLC
LaVergne TN
LVHW011740060526
838200LV00051B/3261